GO Extreme!

BE A PRO WRESTLER

By Lynda Arnez

Gareth Stevens
PUBLISHING

Please visit our website, www.garethstevens.com. For a free color catalog of all our high-quality books, call toll free 1-800-542-2595 or fax 1-877-542-2596.

Library of Congress Cataloging-in-Publication Data
Names: Arnéz, Lynda, author.
Title: Be a pro wrestler / Lynda Arnez.
Description: Buffalo, New York : Gareth Stevens Publishing, [2024] |
  Series: Go extreme! | Includes bibliographical references and index.
Identifiers: LCCN 2023010307 (print) | LCCN 2023010308 (ebook) | ISBN
  9781538287057 (library binding) | ISBN 9781538287040 (paperback) | ISBN
  9781538287064 (ebook)
Subjects: LCSH: Wrestling–Juvenile literature. | World Wrestling
  Entertainment, Inc–Juvenile literature. | WrestleMania–Juvenile
  literature. | Wrestling matches–Juvenile literature.
Classification: LCC GV1195.3 .A7 2024 (print) | LCC GV1195.3 (ebook) |
  DDC 796.812–dc23/eng/20230322
LC record available at https://lccn.loc.gov/2023010307
LC ebook record available at https://lccn.loc.gov/2023010308

First Edition

Published in 2024 by
Gareth Stevens Publishing
2544 Clinton St
Buffalo, NY 14224

Copyright © 2024 Gareth Stevens Publishing

Designer: Ellen Weber
Editor: Kristen Rajczak Nelson

Photo credits: Cover, pp. 1, Arthur Cauty/Shutterstock.com; p. 5 Simon Q/Flickr.com https://creativecommons.org/licenses/by-sa/2.0/; p. 7 Tom Rose/Shutterstock.com; p. 7 Everyonephoto Studio/Shutterstock.com; p. 9 Megan Elice Meadows/Flickr.com; p. 10 Eugene Powers/Shutterstock.com; p. 11 Kathy Hutchins/Shutterstock.com; 13 Miguel Discart/Flickr.com https://creativecommons.org/licenses/by-sa/2.0/; p. 15 Dustin Murrell Broadcast Journalist/Flickr.com; p. 17 Bjoern Deutschmann/Shutterstock.com; pp. 19, 27 Kathy Hutchins/Shutterstock.com; p. 21 BartlomiejMagierowski/Shutterstock.com; p. 23 J.A. Dunbar/Shutterstock.com; p. 25 John Manard/Flickr.com; p. 29 Sam Aronov/Shutterstock.com; Series Art Mind Pixell/Shutterstock.com; Series Art Duda Vasilii/Shutterstock.com; Series Art PegasuStudio/Shutterstock.com; Series Art Scott Webb/Pexels.com.

All rights reserved. No part of this book may be reproduced in any form without permission in writing from the publisher, except by a reviewer.

Printed in the United States of America

Some of the images in this book illustrate individuals who are models. The depictions do not imply actual situations or events.

CPSIA compliance information: Batch #CS24GS: For further information contact Gareth Stevens, New York, New York at 1-800-542-2595.

Ring Dreams	4
About Pro Wrestling	6
Getting in the Ring	10
Go to School	14
Make an Entrance	22
The Big Show	26
Other Income	28
Learn the Lingo	30
For More Information	31
Glossary	32
Index	32

RING DREAMS

As a kid, Matt Cardona dreamed of being a professional wrestler. Matt has since wrestled for some of the best companies in the world. He's known as one of the hardest workers in the business! Are you ready to work hard for your dream too?

PUSHING THE LIMITS

Matt Cardona has also wrestled under the name Zack Ryder. Pro wrestlers sometimes use their own names, but they often have wrestling names.

Matt Cardona

ABOUT PRO WRESTLING

Pro wrestling is part sport, part **performance**. Pro is short for professional, which means someone gets paid to do a job. Pro wrestlers are paid by wrestling companies. Their job is to put on a show that may include wrestling and doing **promos**.

PUSHING THE LIMITS

Amateur wrestling is the sport done by teams at schools and at the Olympics. Some pro wrestlers were amateur wrestlers first!

amateur wrestling

The outcome of a wrestling match is **predetermined**. The wrestlers may plan some of their moves. In big companies, like World Wrestling Entertainment (WWE), matches are commonly part of a larger story.

PUSHING THE LIMITS

Pro wrestling is real—and wrestlers can get really hurt. Bryan Danielson had to stop wrestling in 2016 partly because of the number of **concussions** he'd gotten. He came back a few years later!

Bryan Danielson

GETTING IN THE RING

There are many paths to pro wrestling stardom. For some, it's the family business! They might start training for wrestling with their family when they are young. Saraya Bevis wrestled her first match in her family's company in the United Kingdom when she was just 13!

Saraya

PUSHING THE LIMITS

WWE Superstars Roman Reigns and the Usos are part of the well-known Anoa'i wrestling family. Former pro wrestler and actor Dwayne "The Rock" Johnson is too!

Roman Reigns

Dwayne Johnson

Other pro wrestlers start out as fans! Pamela Martinez has talked about her love for watching wrestling when she was young. These wrestlers often have a lot of **passion** for the sport. Without family in the business, they must find ways to train on their own.

PUSHING THE LIMITS

Martinez, known as Bayley in WWE, was good at sports as a kid! Playing sports now is one way you can start working toward being a pro wrestler.

Bayley

GO TO SCHOOL

Many pro wrestlers trained at wrestling schools. These are often run by people who have worked as pro wrestlers themselves! You must be at least 18 to go to most pro wrestling schools. It can cost a lot of money too.

PUSHING THE LIMITS

Pro wrestlers Colby Lopez (current ring name: Seth Rollins), Brian Myers, and Cody Rhodes all run wrestling schools! These businesses are another way these pros make money outside of being in the ring.

Seth Rollins

Wrestling schools teach wrestling moves. They also teach about creating, or making up, a character. A character is who a wrestler will play when part of a wrestling event. They may talk a certain way and have a certain look.

PUSHING THE LIMITS

Some wrestlers have been many different characters. Windham Rotunda has been known in WWE as Alex Rotundo, Duke Rotundo, Husky Harris, Bray Wyatt, and The Fiend!

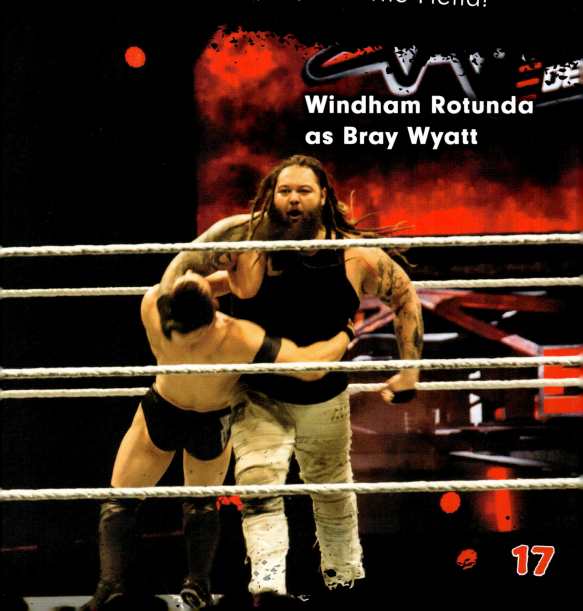

Windham Rotunda as Bray Wyatt

Wrestling schools teach another skill: talking! Some pro wrestling companies tell wrestlers what they're going to say at a show. Others let wrestlers come up with their own promos. Doing promos is as much a skill to practice as anything off the top rope!

PUSHING THE LIMITS

Phil Brooks (ring name: CM Punk) is known as a great talker in the wrestling world. In 2011, he gave a promo that fans still talk about now called the "pipe bomb promo."

At times, big wrestling companies have had **developmental** programs. They are a bit like wrestling schools. For those who have done some wrestling, these programs may be a starting point at the company. Wrestlers in developmental programs may get paid too.

PUSHING THE LIMITS

All wrestling training teaches safety. Not just anyone can jump into a pro wrestling ring. You need to learn how to do moves safely on your own and with others.

MAKE AN ENTRANCE

Once wrestlers know the ropes, they perform! Many start at local **promotions**. They may travel around the country to perform. At first, they won't make much money. As a wrestler starts to make a name for themselves, they will make more!

PUSHING THE LIMITS

Wrestlers can earn money by selling T-shirts, hats, and other gear. At first, many keep other jobs outside of wrestling!

Independent, or indie, wrestling companies are those not owned by a bigger company, like WWE. Wresting on the indies can be a great way to gain fans, sharpen your wrestling and promo skills, and get time in the ring as a pro.

PUSHING THE LIMITS

Some pro wrestlers are happy wrestling for the indies! They want to choose when and where they wrestle. They like being able to work for more than one company at a time.

THE BIG SHOW

For many, success in pro wrestling is signing to a big company, such as WWE or All Elite Wresting (AEW). But their work continues. To get on TV and in matches, wrestlers must come up with good ideas for their character.

PUSHING THE LIMITS

Pro wrestlers often jump from company to company. Mercedes Kaestner-Varnado (known then as Sasha Banks) left WWE in 2022. She first appeared as Mercedes Moné in New Japan Pro Wrestling in 2023!

OTHER INCOME

Pro wrestlers make money to do what they love—wrestle. They may also have **sponsors**, sell fitness programs, or do other work that makes money. And pro wrestling is just the beginning for some performers. Some have gone on to star in big TV shows and movies!

PUSHING THE LIMITS

John Cena has starred in movies and appeared in TV shows as well as continues to wrestle in WWE!

LEARN THE LINGO

card
the list of matches during a wrestling event

face
short form of "babyface," or the hero

finisher
a wrestler's final move that is supposed to beat who they are wrestling against

gimmick
the features of the character a wrestler is playing

heel
the villain

kayfabe
keeping up the idea that wrestling characters and stories are real

push
when a wrestler is being put in more or better matches

spot
moves in a match that have been planned

turn
when a wrestler changes from a face to a heel, or a heel to a face

FOR MORE INFORMATION

BOOKS

Nelson, Kristen Rajczak. *Greatest Wrestlers of All Time*. New York, NY: Gareth Stevens Publishing, 2020.

Proudfit, Benjamin. *Kenny Omega*. New York, NY: Gareth Stevens Publishing, 2022.

Rose, Rachel. *Dwayne Johnson: Actor and Pro Wrestler*. Minneapolis, MN: Bearport Publishing, 2022.

WEBSITES

AEW | All Elite Wrestling News
www.allelitewrestling.com
Follow some of the top wrestlers in the business on the AEW website.

WWE: Official Site
www.wwe.com
Check out all the WWE Superstars here!

Publisher's note to educators and parents: Our editors have carefully reviewed these websites to ensure that they are suitable for students. Many websites change frequently, however, and we cannot guarantee that a site's future contents will continue to meet our high standards of quality and educational value. Be advised that students should be closely supervised whenever they access the internet.

GLOSSARY

concussion: A head injury that affects the way the brain works.

developmental: Having to do with development, or growing and getting better over time.

passion: A great love.

performance: The action of playing a character. To perform is to play a character or to complete an activity or action that requires skill.

predetermined: Decided ahead of time.

promo: What a wrestler says to move the story of a wrestling show forward.

promotion: A group that puts on wrestling shows.

sponsor: A company that gives a person clothes, gear, or money. In turn, the person uses these items and talks about the company to bring attention to it.

INDEX

All Elite Wrestling (AEW), 26
Bayley, 12, 13
Bevis, Saraya, 10, 11
Cardona, Matt, 4, 5
Cena, John, 29
character, 16, 26
CM Punk, 19
Danielson, Bryan, 9
indies, 24, 25
promos, 6, 18, 19, 24
Reigns, Roman, 11
training, 10, 12, 14, 21
World Wrestling Entertainment (WWE), 8, 11, 13, 17, 24, 26, 27, 29
wrestling schools, 14, 15, 16, 18, 20